The commune of our waking

Stuart Ian McKay

Dedication

to sharla, beloved wife…

no longer in exile, we are we.

ISBN: 978-1-990496-13-4

Cover Design: Jessica James

Visit AOS Publishing's website:
www.aospublishing.com

the commune of our waking

in the first of sixty-five declarations a woman
who says *wife* in an evocative manner informs you that
the skills you learned in czarist russia are
not transferable.

furthermore, she continues, *it is now generally
agreed upon that manners in the classical period were
largely determined by lottery.*

*blushing archaeologists report discoveries of
mounds of pottery shards adjacent to disused
temples and the resting spots of shepherds.
on the obverse are the lurid, often ridiculous
descriptions of vulgar practices and expressions.*

the surprising placement of quotation marks
around her pleading *go back and see for your
self* was because her words often had their
firmest foundation in the intentional transference of all
the hesitation ever experienced in one day to the
expansive silence of that other one day when everyone
near her heard a voice intended *just
for me just for me* whisper *if you allow the
non-specific being a child personifies to obstruct
through her provoking essence the most meditative
guide you most surely ever felt buried beneath
your feet at least admit to it.*

okay?

 okay.

perhaps it is tempting to misread any intimate connections to her commentary as if that alone were merely a methodical reinforcement of the fetishisation dispelled after testing oneself against the ghost town of the complexities of personal unworthiness she repeatedly insists upon amending by her more terrestrial spelling of centre.

likewise, it may be grasping after a certain typeface to suggest that gauging a reaction to the following scenario might or might not indicate a particular kind of allegiance with varieties of *working it out well:* it could be any book, but in this case it must be whitman. out of its pages falls a small yellow square of paper. written on one side is *put vitamin e on your scar at night before going to bed.* no aspersions cast into a primal light would lead into the same permitted realm these words use to count down their time, so densify your response before it is too late.

sigh. continue.

in popular imagination, pangea exists as a means of translating and transmitting a better and more fluid series of digressions. to most, such digressions are considered an ancestral memory of a kind of printing as easily lost as it is created, which, when properly used, will allay all fears. glaciation on pangea achieved the same effect, but it stripped away the lectures of history a little too well, and all that remained was a generally illegible postscript too corrupted to be thought of as a decent, dependable source for even a private epic story.

but all this is the shape of

longing. she tells you. *hold up a*

handful of earth to your ear.

tell me i'm lying.

at rest on the coastline of living
reasonably well

anyone? anyone?

a concrete pillar. a recommendation for a new
kind of prayer. the solidity between these two.

proposing that what remains of memory is evidence
of a carefully recollected abandonment structured
upon an expressionless december in athens and a
champion in the harbour shouting *save! save!*

in the streets, in the cafés, the clamour of youthful
apologists clashing with retirees acutely in the know.

your friend's conception of frustration.

yours.

saying *i'll be right over. we'll share what we have, be
happy with only a campfire and a grey sky.*
some starry thing shining moderately well.

a version of an unwritten canto

your now becoming aware of the
advantageous possibilities of repeating
first to yourself then to some stranger
at a dull, sparsely attended gallery
opening these highlighted sections of
your personal apocrypha and their
corporeality consistent with a year's
worth of thwarted passions...

your having collapsed onto the
strange orange leather couch in
front of the garish sculpture of
a clown failing to do a backflip.
the free but terrible wine served
in an ugly glass you would
later dream about...

your wanting to wrap that
exquisite powerlessness around
your head like one of those
tinfoil hats you are often
compelled to make...

that glorious long-lasting diamond
gleam! sequins pasted to the cover of
the journal you carried in your
backpack all through junior high...

the zipper, you thought, was stronger
than the great wall. every word
a brick, a border to any invader.

soon you became the garrison your
childhood had threatened you with.

but that one fatalistic day...

libby, your closest cousin. her
friends. laughing. pointing.

the two of you, not speaking again
until the victoria day long week
end in second-year university.

her tent was origami under the
sticky, heavy snow. could she stay
with you, use the extra sleeping
bag she knew you always had?

the motion of this entry being
sealed up again sounded like the one
you both knew had, in fact, happened.

she unburdened her old silence in front
of you, hoping it would radiate potency like
a revivalist's meeting, but before any sacred
text was opened or either of you shook
with a life-altering frenzy, you said,

libby, *I once suspected all my previous*
rainbows would lead me here to this
very spot, because maybe they were an
attempt to emphasise something more,
something other than a lost reconciliation that
my blank face, your blank face could
ever redecorate. don't think we're too
old now, nor too young, that kaleidoscopes
are irrelevant. peer inside if you can.
say sorry every time you're blinded
briefly. come up with a name for
what happens to you.

just leave me out of it.

look for a cactus in a jar

... um... so...

what did happen during your
short modernist summer?

as soon as you put on your good
grey dress to celebrate its trope-like
dawning, we should have known you
meant business. you held out a

non-neutral metaphorical hand
then scooped up all the leavings of
every critic we had ever befriended.

this has been the best day!

you told us. still, weeks went by

without a single response to our
one centralising question: in all the
time you were with us, when exactly
did you first sense that your inter
connectivity had begun to give off
the smell of a big box of crayons?

more to the point, why does the lion
roaring at you from across *that* chasm

work as well as it does at situating
the kind of idealistic love you
really, truly want to exemplify in thought, word
and deed? oh, by the way,

who was it who coloured in his
cardboard mane? you? a student?

no matter. if there is a trespass

in our craving to entice out of ambiguity
these frantically speculated-about modes
of authenticity we aspire to parade around in, why are
we aware of it so rarely?

a person's soul, you revealed to us, *will
pencil in the right circle on the test
only fifty percent of the time. the rest
is just guesswork huddled between
periods of grandiosity no amount of
advice could nationalise.*

not now. not ever.

we listened. wow, did we listen.

you can tell. right?

going down your list of thematic residencies

certainly, here in the apparent absolutism of
the outer rim amongst the supernovae and other
regulars, there is something strange, something remote
not even the oppsarooni of your whacked-out
prana is strong enough to resist.

that said, what startles you the most — and this
is evident in your carl sagan-like stare of
advanced, abandoned inquiry — is how in this place
of eternal, binding resolution your well-functioning
self-editing circulatory system perpetuates its
many astonishing diagnostic quandaries.
so, you sit down. someone named edna hands you
her print version of diversity, and now, maybe, just
maybe, you know why you were witness to the best, the
longest of any cartoon saturdays worth wallowing
in and the tremendous sensation of those
too few augusts stevie wonder sang you through.

you do feel it all over. you do.

you. do.

also, if you owe anything to those special persons
who help you manoeuvre the complexities you
barely face — family, friends, librarians, book
sellers, cabbies, servers — it is this anxiety erupt-
ing from stuttering replies to queries only they
make after watching other crowds argue
about what other crowds argue about.

yes, the day will come when you
will relax in a dentist's office and
not be kicked out, not be sent home.

afterwards you will want to take down notes
about where you've been, what you've been doing,
but today, today there's no time because today
time curves back into itself. today.

but who corners you into your humanity?
who says *you* better than you?

who's writing *this* down? you have work to do,
the ability to do all things to repletion.

salt and light. you say

salt and light.

the rest, as they say,

is

the sound poem you aspire to be

for steve gillespie 1962-2004, victoria poet

breath-hold ebb the length of this day intoning

across the shoal

landed you have landed the dock
collects all the immovability an instant
is real inside all intimated appearing things
somewhere a history attends

opens up drifts

like a text shorn off a text a distant friend
gazes back

sees you

his fragile *go go*

uttered as adornment possessed because of

your calming

here i'm here

but say say this much of what an incompleteness is say it
is elegiac, artifact-like, nearly a voice, but one lacking
any allegiance to the apostrophe it longs to recover

 for such a space such a sensation a greatness

nootka

no ooot kaaaa

aaa a he his *nooo oo t kaa* poem he his *no ooot kk a*
poem he his poem he

as unspoken as departed as from an autumn that
autumn you your poems shared those sea and ocean
poems those beach grass poems those poems in hard
stone winter poems those autumns that autumn poems
before he his poem his poem

before he *aaa* he his poems before *a*
 a

broken long vocal line a *do you want to hear this one
stu i wrote it last week at annie's after the reading* a
mediated concession lessening such a weight such a
shape

a such a such a

a such such a

such a now sensed now say said so now say so say so so
so sensed a sympathy so sensed
a printing imprinted say so so such a

flat black grey beach stone so say so say so a flat black
grey beach stone so say so varied a say so so varied
waves wave these last these last varied waves at last this
this concord is at last at last so vivian calls to say his
heart hearts a heart goes go go a shape such a weight
closes closes off and is lightly light and words and words
and
do not shape this lightly words do not close off his
heart's closing close

o   *o*

o   o   *o*

                o

o

                o   *o*

o

a

o   *o*

your stellar equivalency really got me down last night

the temporal need the fundamental gift of faith
of a small house a different part of the city

the day you move in peeling wallpaper splotches of
paint *pink yellow orange blue*

no one, not even you, explaining why the
complimentary plenitude of this illustrious
bursting forth has come to mean that a
particular type of darkness nears its
less dissonant end but

 is this why is this where

you make an account of the individual
difficulties of your relational self

 did i close the door

 is the
 window
 open

and comprehended quantifiable is this merely accepted
prefix of a potential solitude the only redemptive
melody resonant at the glowing tear-like core of an
expanding universe one you can reasonably measure by
the number of girl and or boyfriends the cool kids
acquired during high school

you do not know

you were not one of them

your assumptions based on an operative
normality are wrangled into a corral at bedtime

and by now you are certain

the architecture of a gate is an ancient
well-meaning system of putting all your stuff
away like a good little boy

nighty-night sleep well

now and only now in such and such a place
peace brokered like a doctrine with the causes
non-causes of this resplendent morning now
and only now in such and such a place do you
rest your coffee cup on the deeply purposed
linoleum counter those incised canyons where
you wish you were minimised an atom floating
along those high walls that less aesthetic sky

like forgiveness you say the audacious looking
neither to the left or to the right a progression
of accepted plurality the time knowing takes

though soon the stylised confirming synthesis of *yes*
and a privately rehearsed day's diminution   likened to
its last nearest narrative best

though soon the involving the honest texture of *i do i*
will stated out as atmosphere into the room those
various less freed things

though soon an abruptly burning bright   disc overhead

 blazing after what it too inherits

a love poem you pray over during a time of exile

in the country we are emigrating towards
we will witness how the patterns of the old
superimpose themselves over those of the new.

as soon as we settle ourselves in, we discover
that what we really want is to feel all the energy
of everything we have ever left behind infuse
itself into and then rapture up the best
achievements of the dialect you and i
alone have learned to speak.

just as we predicted would happen, the
confused people going out for brunch
the morning after our going-away party
will be talking about us.

did you see them! what a display! what a to-do!

like a pair of exuberant butterflies
holidaying on a heat-beaten rock in tunis,
they were majestical in their combined
non-need of harnessing a single photon of
the sun's life-enhancing, nostalgia-making
insularity in their dear oh dearie me oh
so precious, ever-elegant, purpose-welcoming
spectacle giving off of wings.

nobody but they could access or
experience the hidden grammar they
perfected in the flourish of their
interpretive dance.

turning, turning,

they occupied the entirety of whatever
room they happened to be in. and from them
wafted great, unpredictable traditions of
sky-air-not the banalifying, othering sort, but,
those that accessorise the chanted time limits
of celibacy from obstructionist noise and activity.

remember? we did that too. once.

unlike those two, we did not meet quota.

we lacked the foresight they had, to set up
a series of crystal vases leading to our front
door. the arc of our footsteps was neither
nubile or illusory.

we instructed nobody.

what did i do with my beer?

it's true. all they said.

we are the landscape they fantasised about.

we are the portion of a place our friends
will hysterically age themselves inside.

i told you as much when we were walking
home from the party and, giggling, adopted
the park bench as our own. you buttoned
and unbuttoned your coat in-between
each snicker. i searched through my pockets,
howling, saying, *my pen, my pen, who's got
my pen?* nothing was more evident than us
that day, we agreed, and nothing could ever be
as easily taken away. we knew we were indebted
to songs about finalaties, defined and redefined,
until their clarity, sharpened like a tool,
struck a hard surface. a boulder maybe?

sparks would fly. something like a bell
would sound. someone would do something.

when it happens, we'll know.

we'll know.

all points of contact on a large indoor lake

though on enceladus   though small

a

rotational force

the question of water
a grey and white crater

contrapuntal grey   contrapuntal white

though your lover   though her dream

yours

though one night   an absence   the question

of water

though a small rotation

a

contrapuntal force

your grandmother gives you for a gift a book of the world's last great mysteries

in those provided-for days, it had become
necessary to produce a new model for
seclusion and abandonment. the great era
of parental documentarians still had some
vitality to it, and the low hum of a black
wheel spooling up real-life discord and impassioned
ambiguity could yet prophesy hitherto
unargued for pleasures of the bodily realm.

the astute clued in fairly quickly to the
work ahead. theirs was a lived experience,
and they proclaimed that nostalgia must be
more than the privileging of one memory
over another. they thought for a time and
half a time, and soon drew a comparison to
gauguin's best practices. *observe the suggested*
potential of his lover's acquiescence.

note the deep well of her eyes, the
luxuriant slope of her hips, her bronze skin,
which only moments ago shared its contemplative
passivity with that warm strand of beach.

were that this exotic bonding
 of elements

its language a friction of images,

an expressive tension of afterthought.

as in: *let us be as heroic as he! may our hands be as mighty as his!*

our lips as well proportioned, as wings! and release!

release!

release!

as in: a secret read as an absolute from a distance.

you tell two friends. they tell two friends.

as in: what this tourism does. to a man. to a woman. to a child.

as in: *that nectar. its scrumptious fragrance wafting towards us like an escape.*

a nearly forgotten holiday? a one remarkable flower clutching the branch of an ancient tree? a day's worth of words when none needed any kind of ending?

but what was it made us recall a sailor stranded in such a place? did he, a week into his breaking away, march up those newly discovered steep stone steps — that brutal interior pyramid! — only to have his blood dry and crust there until it could only be ignored?

and what was that in his left hand? a papaya?

green and yellow-orange, like a bird's plumage.

its vision joined with the air.

at least when we said megalithic we really tried to mean it. we knew and know without ceasing that catastrophe is a gerund in cellular form, and its broadening in the body is the evidence of all folklore. we feel what we realise. although there may be a randomness to these references, can we ponder anew what way there is for us and for those closest to us to contextualise this montage?

being as we are both gauguin and the sailor, our quest for a resting place for our regret is ever at odds with our habit of rushing forward with all our belongings, like props for the big show, and we stumble-bumble past grandiosity despite the many sharp warnings given us.

the syllables of such warnings do come at a high cost. in appearance and delivery, they are crispier than salt crystals when exposed to a perfect source of light, but they inevitably attract the sort of solemn work they conclude.

now, shaken...

who goes for us? whom shall we send?

.

the invocation of a rhythm into the body

awooshawooshawoosha awoosha

a blankspace a

before you go

a your coat your shoes
a *this is is not* loss

isisisisis

is

a domesticity
is somewhere

channelled to an outside and its ringing in the   ears is
akin to an echo of a chant's dispersing those welcomes
that have lent it breath

think also of an icicle on this day
each epoch — making drip

for her for you

do not hush this littleness; do not ask why

and the word

send
imprinted in the new snow

behind you behind you
yesterday's gravity answered in your uplifted opened
hands

what falling is when it fills caws caws the crow

*gogosogosososogogosogoishesheishesheisheigogoshei
sosheshesogosheshegosogoshesheigoso*

she she i she

but shade that glaze in ice
caution numbs

but that was a forever ago *she she i she i she* that
sonorous surface crack

the puddle satisfies
passes the test

like an orchestra is precise

she she she i go she i she

but take this private sanctity an oath to its dwelling in
you you're yours *a breath a br e a th a br e ath a* what
more could sanction this ambient sculpturing
now then a later page-bound day whose lyric like paper
crinkles at its edges

abreathabreathabreatha

a say a way i say i saw a way i say i saw a way i
say i saw i say a way a way i saw i say i saw i say
i saw a way i saw a way i say i saw a way

an image its bettering silence there

hidden again its transitory stating

its stating seen

lighter now this visitation ended

the soul's solitary ideation the principal
source of an escape it dignifies

your *enough* sung by a flake of snow

the seven muted suns that make up yesterday

chrism glisten. the rare and diligent silence of this
quieted-down hymn. were waiting — ever and always a
choreography of waiting.

now covetous of the removal of allusions, you
press, from one onto the weave of the finest paper.

the small birch bark box you seal it into rests
a whole season on the snowbank then takes
your childhood far away. there is a mountain,
a chorus of peaks. a letter. a letter. a
letter. a letter. a letter. a letter. a letter.

a mass. whose eyes will host, exalt?

the alleluia of the renunciates

*voice come glory come do not lack a voice glory glory
come do not lack a voice come voice mouth glory come
do not lack a voice come glory come come voice eye
glory do not lack a voice eye on stone glory do not lack
a voice glory hand in water glory do not lack a voice
glory glory do not lack do not lack a voice foot on grass
glory do not lack a voice glory do not lack a voice glory
air upon stone upon hand upon the eye upon the foot
upon the grass air of mouth glory do not lack a voice
glory glory come*

glory voice the grass glory voice the stone

*glory voice air and water glory voice the   mouth the
eye*

come come come voice voice voice

your glory

come

you are become entangled with your
textual opposite

hypatia

my most beloved, most confused poet, i have
written elsewhere of how time is the surest tutor.

distance, geography, the variability of historical
events, the malleability of cultural standards are
immaterial, porous, when set against the fact of
a candle burning down to its nub, or a water
clock, dry, depleted of purpose at day's end.

face this.   find strength.   time cares nothing
for you.   when it does arrive, do not flee.

poet, from my library to yours, from my sea-bound
city to yours, perched on plain and mountainside,
i offer these few words, these few thoughts.

pharos, as you know, is big, dauntingly
mysterious, but still a beacon for those who
need it. little do they care what forces within
cause it to cast out light. pharos does. that is
all they need to know.

they feel.   they see.   they proceed.

why are we so different than they?

poet

well… alright… experience illustrates the
nobility of stumbling around in the dark.

the back of a cave can be the same
kind of conveyance as a ship's hold.

in a previous letter, you comment on how
you clambered through one of my handwritten
poems. my ruinously messy, stark black
letters on often tea-stained paper remind
you of bushes burning away like fodder
in a furnace.

the passionate transformation of an
organic integrity into a pile of ashes…

but, hypatia, from each word i hang
colour and light to lead the way. lanterns at
carnival, if you will. a defence against
death and mediocrity is vigour and meaning.
go is like an exit from and an entry into
a pulsing heart. and afterwards, everyone
shouts *i went there! me too! so did i!*

i stayed!
i will again!

hypatia

i see that the solitude you discover and
nurture in your poems has done you some good.

do continue.

meeting as we do in the seclusion and silence
of our work, we are both of us travellers
to the same unknown, unknowable? shore.

wonderment will be our guide. it is he who led
us together. what satisfaction there is
on those mornings when i find your newest
letter scrolled up in my library's copy of
herodotus, or those afternoons when you
come across my response, pressed as it is
between pages of your notes and edits.

this happens.   that is all.   there is no
greater why than circumstance.

our place is there.

poet

i may need that.   let me write it down.

my companion to these troubling days, it occurs
to me that the condition of remaining vulnerable to an
idea has a shape, a substance. it is a thing anyone can
grasp.   it is an experience worth having.

take tarkovsky, for example. in solaris, life or
what seems to resemble life, gathers itself around
traumatised men and a woman struggling to revive
their answers to the causal presence joining them
together.   they want to remember.

in their needfulness rests their humanity.

this, then, is the true island in the film.

but, where do they go?   where?

hypatia

obviously, this crowd has not entirely learned
through the senses or the memory what an alphabet
does, how it explodes action into expression,
and, thus, aids in resistance to the void.

imagine a letter, carved either from wood or
ivory. do you have it? is it proof to you yet?
now, see this: all the people of the world, sliding
gracefully down upon its face

there is room, poet... room for everyone...

poet

once again, hypatia, you lead me to abstraction.

as a poet, i recognise the alluring utility of the
ephemeral, but the energising apparent is what
most draws me in these days.   i mean, it's cold
outside.

self-doubt is like ice. i'm slipping on everything. all i
want to do is go home. i'm tired and hungry.

the least you could do is give me a candle.

hypatia

poet, please calm down.   as before, you're thinking
too much about the wrong thing, and in the wrong
manner. if you'll allow me to help, my argument
could lessen the direness and gloom of your own doing.

you yourself have witnessed how a poem, as all things
also do, will grow from discrete particles to a more
robust form; from yet one word or sound or
image builds the next. a word, then, is a genesis
for other worlds; it is a place of belonging for those
who choose to reside there. how they choose to do
so is revealing. here, poet, it is here i see you best:
hard at work. this is where the action is,
where you always are.

i am baffled.
how adept you are at forgetting the pattern
of your liberty. why is it you wallow in this
boring psychic disquiet, when the way out is
so wonderfully clear, not only to me, but also to you?

please recall one of your first letters:
in frenzied detail, you describe the triumph
of a deeply productive long day spent writing.
i have no trouble seeing you perched in the middle of
your room.
around you on the floor,
like a wheel, are hundreds of sheets of paper:
notes, edits, ideas sketched out, nearly-completed
poems, those approaching abandonment and those
set free to the wind and the world, drawings, pictures,
books and books, empty cups, full wine glasses,
bowls and plates of food gone cold.

and you! you, poet! considering the
picturesque implications of the scene…

as grand, as virtuous and as splendid,
as colossal, as he of rhodes!

you ask for a candle. i give you a torch.
we ought to remember that the colossus

stared out to sea. what were those relentless
ceaseless waves to that impregnable dignity?

imagine that reflection…

broadly spreading upon the rippling
waters, calming all who drew near…

shadows, caught in the bouncing light
of the tides, reassert the ocean's depths…
no?   still you do not understand.

a creative life is a spectacle.   images mass
with images.   one recedes.   one dominates.
one emerges alongside one about to vanish.
one crystalises, one dims to nothingness.
an artist, haunted by what he has or hopes
to have envisioned, aches after an authentic
exposition to guide him to a frontier he
cannot possibly predict. the matter of going
is wholly in his hands. what does he require
of an audience he may never meet?

approval? praise? what are they to him?

the colossus stared out to sea.
myself…i am transfixed.

what other name could i summon,
what other name is proportionate to,

this…going in?...we each crave after?

….all those overlapping pages of
overlapping words, touch, caress, resist
again, caress again, those maze-like,
mosaic-like words and letters forming,
embracing, brave new variants of
provocative, joyful, outrageous,
life-giving, declarative acts.

go in, poet, to this *going in*!   go in!

poet

let me shake off the debris.

clear my eyes.

be clean.

there is *that* somewhere i am
literate enough to voyage towards,
a discovery i can occupy even
as it occupies me.

why, alone in my waiting,

in the urgency of my different
world's coming,

do i stay   a willing stranger?

a colonist?   and when did i
first suspect that

to walk in unfamiliar fields,
to feel such a warm, wet soil –
whirling, curling between my toes –
to drink water of a less acrid taste
to stand, melancholic, before a vista,
incapable of retreating inside,

would enliven only me?

is this how i am safe?
there! a mountain, a glacier!
a euphoria of a kind! and, there!
no greying critic's greying voice,
muttering back to me the long
lamentation of my eroding
defeatism. suddenly, this is an
ancient idleness. the vigilant rejoice

now, because in this their vivid tableaux -
all those preparations given to those props and
excesses, all those animate and inanimate objects
they crowd their tender speech and actions around
like a bulwark against ruination and decay,
all that inhabitable security captured by this
day, that day's chantworthy orthodox littleness,
all the confident satisfaction of saying *say,*
don't you see how your saying says what
you see?, all those necessary descriptive and
non-descriptive dictates of some bossy
specified memory that a formidable somebody
not yet encroached upon, all the prescient
density of a welcoming hope welcoming you
home, all the *it's a.....it's a, isn't it?* anyone
declaims over and over again for as long as it
takes to source a truthful music from an
apostrophe – with chutzpah, with gusto, they
acknowledge the submissive qualities of a

refusal, as if it were a pile of pale dust and
the rest of the world were a

still sharply outlined though certainly austere
structure echoing back to its printed word's aesthetic
heritage various types of cyclically remitted
dream – like states' a sibling's argument over
that momentarily generated space where regret
is disallowed entry; an acclaimed valuing of an
exotically derived means of detente best symbolised
through a well-painted wooden wheel, which, not
surprisingly, will only turn at sunrise; a lone
practitioner of the art of laudatory divination who
bellows out, but not to anyone in particular, *i need to
see a different world-happening i need to see a different
world-happening i need to see a*; a couple who, after
a week's long fight discern a defensible philosophy
out of scuff marks near the front door, the clatter of
dishes in the sink, books closed, opened, closed again
before being set down on the nightstand; a poet
birthed
in the *ektheiazo* of his late summer's needful
solitude, maintains, confers, conceals his vauntworthy
resistance with *what actions! what designs!* – which,

like any now definable, answerable
thing, the electrifying few seconds
following its having been translated by
and displayed through the deeply
recessed language of a privately

apprehended mythos; like the strict
economy of a melody – that long and
well-reasoned out ancestral concern
like the perfected, completed context of
story, say, for example, of a woman
who, responding to the sandpapery voice of
a stranger, asking from the back of a poorly
lit café, *are you lost?*, like asking if
she does walk towards him, only to
say *yes*, and wondering if are we not there too?

hypatia

poet...hidden here in this shroud
realm of your likeness – are you now contented?
are you now attended to? – can you do
anything more than endure that conflict,
that hurling together, that tearing apart
of those many varied words and images,
that catalogue of allusions?

is this distracted, discordant murmuring
the best sound of your better voice?

specifics?

yes.   specifics...

latch on.   consider this:

a critic, especially one as sizable as yours,
acts like a patriot, seizing hold of whatever
he opposes; where no fault exists, he finds,
manufactures many; like a luridly-minded
man, he adores, wildly pursues cataclysm.

meanwhile, despite the plague of his dreadful
fictions, better ones than he achieve images
from air; words, they cradle gently on hand,
like skittish birds, made suddenly calm.

whose power is superior?
whose liberty more enduring?

he might say…you might claim:
look and know! his merest ornamentation is
an obscurantist's most unpardonable luxury,
an offensive obsession, that shames poets
and poetry back into the closet of
inopportune, theatrical showiness.

arranged as it is as an addendum to the array
of sensations it may or may not contain, and,
thereby, express, his poetry – every word, line,
image and thought-models a certain kind of
conceit which can only be named after
the material it fails to take on.

this poet welcomes no one. readers are
cautioned to not lose themselves in his verse.
there is no trail of breadcrumbs leading them
back out from his malaise-laden plains
of looming aesthetic stupor.

no, all he gives – to us, to himself – is his
inability, his incapacity? to bridge distances
between those yearning, longing souls whose
most basic, ardent, authentic wish is to
shed the collective skin of the turgid
self-loathing brought on by this age's
perpetual spiritual, cultural and intellectual

defeatism and banal, deadening uniformity.
poet!   lift your head!

let the scales fall from your eyes!

is it truly as you imagine?

is it just as you fear?

are you fated to process through this
dark, awesome tyrannical fantasyworld alone?

you tell me you feel as defenceless, as
fragile as a stick figure in a reed boat.
you despair your work will have no
more of an impact upon the world than
dust blown against a pane of glass, and
that your days on this earth are as
immaterial as a whisper in an arid land.

escape, poet.   escape yourself.

no other force can dominate you
if you forbid it entry. the golden age
you crave after is yours, but you
must believe you can call it your own.

even a comma is a beginning.

allow that your work describes your life.

suppose a poem is a proving ground for anxieties,
stray thoughts and ill-considered actions.

might a poem also exalt private discoveries
of latent ecstasies and private victories?
escaping back into some from of personal
escape, a poem is a perpetually imperfect,
incompleted event, but it is a shrine for men and
women desperately wishing to expose themselves
to a vast, wildly instinctual need for an expressive
ideal based in more than an actual source of hope than
in the estrangement of various souls brought
about by an affecting but unsatisfying solitude.

tell me, my poet...who comes to such and
such a place of exotic mystification?

is it you?   is it me?   who then?!

tell me, poet!   hurry!   what's keeping you?!

poet

hypatia, these are dark corners you have
led me into, and i have no words to see
beyond where they confine me.

hypatia, my distant one, light and shadow
fall from a surface in equal measure.

both conceal.   both expose.

who am i, what am i to you that
you should penetrate, by thought and
word, my negligible calm with pleas to
see myself clearly? what thing do you
hope to author, to perform within me?

where i go, why do you follow?

i seek a gratifying, ordering solitude
where i can armour my soul against the
smothering excesses of these days.

i wait to surrender my imagination
to its themes, feel them reverberate
through me.

last week, wanting the ephemeral, i
left my home, walked and walked on
streets I hadn't *really* seen in years.

it was hours before i stopped to rest.

soon worn out, i sat on a park bench.

in front of me, warmed by the permeating
sun, was a large marble sculpture.
i thought i knew this work well. it had always
brought me joy and satisfaction. on this day, though,
i only felt disturbed, as if i had been summoned
into the presence of a living thing, murmuring
remain   resist   .

i wanted to adopt that permanence, have it inside
me, to share its solidity: that luminous, creamy
stone, those countless blue-grey veins scattered
throughout like galaxies; the well-defined wrinkles
of the figure's hands, the tree-trunk like whorls
of his one extended finger; perched there, a bird,
the deft modelling of its wing feathers; what it is
to soar, to befriend the sky; what it is to root
an idea in place, in abandonment to place. what
hypatia, was i missing? neglecting to notice?

i went home afterwards, looked at my poems,
those in infancy, those out in the world.
they, those words, were like a crowd of celebrants,
offering up their need. to me? to anyone? to you?

say yes. hypatia, if you can, say yes.

hypatia

poet, pause before a different pedestal.

recall the first words you sent me: *our
meeting, our long association and correspondence
have all the probability and believability of
a shoddily written popularist drama.*

what scene, vivid and life-giving, is carved there?
what bids you welcome? how do you allow
yourself licence to enter comradeship with
the materiality of its solitude?

like an exile gazing out to his dreamlife, do
you only describe an exotic silence? must you
imagine it is solely distance you have learned to
conquer? what, then, is the rubble of a civilisation
at doomsday to you? are superior perspective,
finer sensations, a culmination of contradictions –
each responding to the other until peace assumes
a recognisable, pleasing form – part of an idea, or
the soul of an idea, that provokes, motivates
your going in, your coming out of the locale you
desperately wish to identify within yourself?

when you do arrive…there…how will you know?

it is no deception to say that, eroded from the edifice
of an abandoned temple, a pebble is lost to the
surrounding plain. it is appropriate to claim that
a senseless man, facing a blank wall, chains
himself to a burden impossible to adorn.

it becomes necessary to state such facts.

here, in this region where language is gloss to
loneliness,
it becomes helpful to form a stillness,
a silence, around the notion that doubt, when
unquestioningly venerated, mocks memory and thus
protect the virtue both generate in dutifully alive souls.

no?   you disagree?

poet, it need not follow that i, by lessening the
grip of one world, should favour the tightening
noose over the neck of its companion.

it is not a theory, it is not a daydream; it becomes
inevitable: few are they who augur their fate from
the work given them to leave as a signature upon the
cosmos. but, it is not for these ones to know the
near infinite how's and why's of strangers in far off
days who may partake in these choice gifts.

in a way you understand, i will illustrate.

you may sometime suppose that long before a word is
conceived, long before its location is assured of on
paper,
it creates a gap, an interval in history, in which the
multitude of possibilities it both negates and invigorates
are cast, shadow-like upon the world.

as if truthful to the things it represents, as if accurate to
the causes of the actions it cannot escape mimicking,
your hand in that very shadow feels that warm,
labouring
far-off sun.

you may discover a stranger sitting nearby.
her hand enters the shadow, joins with yours.

are you faithful to this stranger's need?
do you value what you offer her? how do you
          thank her for being *here*?

you tell her of a library burnt away from the earth.
she tells you of a poem she has found, rising upwards
from the
page, of its prominence over everything she witnesses
and
remembers, of how the experience of it makes her recall
her
lover, the landscape they shared, gloried in discovering.

poet, this moment is written into you. into anyone.
into me.   i read you, reading me.

your words….known, unknown…i return to you.
they continue.   somewhere.

who says you better than you?

in these provided for days, channeled, elegiac
and artifact-like to an outside glory, you make
an account of the individual difficulties of your
relational self.   but, that one fatalistic day!

comprehended, quantifiable, blazing after what
it too inherits, it is some starry thing, shining
moderately well. you do feel it all over, you do,
you do.   with its radiating potency, it's trope-
like dawning, you do!   you do!

the apparent absolutism of the dialect you
and i have alone learned to speak, situates us
in the kind of idealistic love that is the
furthermore of someone's sixty five declarations.

*the solidity between these working out well
rhythms of the body is the stylised confirming
synthesis of yes and a privately rehearsed
diminution likened to its last, its nearest
narrative best.*

tell me I'm lying.

just leave me out of it.

all the usualness of want and its many
barren whispers of prophecy

symperasma

a poem in balance   *thus translated*

(a)   thrafsmata   *akin to*   *(b) diatonic*

(a)   *but observe*   *remember*

it may well be true that it takes an aware man or
woman thirty years to build a life worth having

a cloud   its smooth passing over the face of a
mountain   a child's upturned hand to what his
eyes claim as his own

                   an appeal to desire like an exorcism

for some is a calling out for a newer kind of conversion
a
more complementarian   more innovative light   not
the dulling glow of an opposing sun

        but an expanse   exposed

    imagine an attentive man

as he does most days   his is active in the public

square   he has all the necessary items for a decent

rigorous   valorous life   the market is full   always

his friends   family   his wife   involve him in community

his work goes well   is widely admired

            however   permeating the soft edge of memory

        an assortment of abstractions and he
struggling

            seeking calm   against their potency

now   it is an impressive thing to consider   will he

maintain the proper discipline of wisdom   and
transform

but one haunting idea into a useful teaching

how might he ponder   how might we ask

can he himself know

that to go forwards   is to abandon

but   provided

we consider   provided we inhabit the space our
consideration

is   we may envision our man   always and forever

a stranger

his days   he   presented there before an

enlivening signal coming from a more distant

opposing shore   having journeyed forth   he

is apprehended by   curious about

the startling pink and white hues of a remarkable
seashell

the undenied dignity of a flattened   grey-green stone

glistening   smooth

those

          centuries of tides

a stark pretense   he   inured against the path
he

    carries   moulds his hand around

    that wordless   word-seeking thing

living as it were we   like an audience to the scene
aware

unaware   of the gift we wish to receive   anticipate

a delirious silence

         much like that of a bell
         about to sound out
   in the darkness

            we

            he

  in

this lusting after catastrophe's private sorrow   our
glamourising of its isolationist decadence

knowing full well

the optimum way forward to that world where disaster need

not bind disaster lies in accepting the ecstatic incompleteness of

a gradual   an intentional   surrendering of customs

standards   principles   some are enamoured with but fail

to respond to meaningfully except by reckoning with the

opposite of what they tend to affect
                          while we still

                          have breath

                          how is it we loathe

        intimacy with such thinking   preferring

        the sure jubilance of decay   the sensibility

            buried in language
perverted from its better root

a question still lingers

its intricacies   mysterious

though not so foreign

as to be deemed unapproachable

like a reprimand from childhood   accepted or

not   its utility   evokes those dreamy glories

those previous solitudes   we rage to keep safe

and   we are compelled to wonder

if we atrophy inside our   willful vanishing away from
our

purposeful neglecting of   the untamed   then mourned
after

expressions that once were mere familiarities to us

must we   now estranged from those summoned forth
wounds
endure their legacy a second a third   time   forth

as we too often end up doing

with other equally ponderous calamities

for we now afflicted

the portion of these verses

an ancient   still unnamed poet

apprenticed to the brightly unfolding dawn

our share in its warmth   a garment

for other   less radiant days

in a far off age   it may be considered an act of

bravery to suggest we are not wholly sure of

what we think by endurance   exposing ourselves to

the discomfort words convert us to   we will journey

forth through their real influence as one   but if

we can conceive of an image   made perfect by

experiencing its climate of justification   let us

reason out a suitable scene   its neglected light

to humiliate us accordingly   do we see

a proud young man   his limbs   luminescing
his defiant smile

rowing his boat to shore

would that it were always so

we must see them

they who witness   who exalt his coming   their fears

having been contended with   loosened to the sky

            feast   sing   dance

the true   the noble day

we must see them   know they

tear warm bread in greeting   drink cool water from jugs

buried shallow in sand   pluck morsels of honeycomb
out of an

old dish   arrayed as if it were a mound of amber
glory

along with them in their bliss

an aroma of glad sacrifice   fish bake on the fire's coals

a new colony   its founding   commemorated

we talk of this good generation   but do the visions we

confine it in   define it by

defeat not only they who call it home   but us too

        does it fail us   this comparison

        are we wise to glean   after its flawed
form
        some sharper mention of a superior truth

        or do we acquiesce   doubt gathered

        there before us   like a trophy

should we discern in those slight wrinkles around his
eyes

        disaster   ruination   mayhem

conjure up visions of drought-ridden farmlands

of a once esteemed city

earthquake   plague   inferno
          pestilence

and   from these   foretell the primal source of private
wars

  a child   the stone he hurls at a friend   the heat

  coming off that language   broken between them

like a pot   pulled impatiently from the kiln

the inexperienced   unobservant novitiate

the fault of his abrupt lack
having expressed this much   it becomes

appropriate to recall a certain sister of thebes

she   ever a pilgrim to her duty   obedient to

an auspicious signal   an insistent idea   pursues

its spent   its failing trajectory

the ornament of her   of our   obsession

secreted away there in the carnage   the

multiplicity of hazards of that now legendary debris

what then draws her   anyone   forward

is it a dull thud to a dulling earth   or

is it a melodious clattering upon and amongst sharp

stones   hollowed out branches and bleached

broken bones littering a small valley

a muffled irrelevancy   or an

alluring invitation

who goes out to see

who may   sometime   ask

would that he

our proud young one   cradled there   now in the

suddenly truthful solitude of that broad land

of personal undoing

                        face us   facing him

were that all the words set down amongst us

those not yet despatched into the valley as a

dying echo   not humiliate their grandiosity the

space they are meant to fashion   would that we

attend well   having been taught well   those

burdens brought to us by listening

against disaster   this my private prologue

if born to condemnation   must i stay my tongue

refrain from indelicate rumour   act forever

as my own chorus   or   better they   my

friends not suspect my motives   arrayed

here as it were   in defiance of its

frightful   unapproachable margins

how like a rope slung around my neck   how like rocks

tied to my ankles   is the sight of my companions
arrayed there   languid indolent   in the warm sand
the feast over   youth's wine drunk to dreaminess

are they now   must they always be   doomed to only
neglect

this summoning of conscience   the reinventing of the
mind

that is the wonderment of cause and affect   interpreted

revealed   represented inside the images a mollifying
slumber

calls forth   those triumphal processions   those
devastating

calamities   those feats of outlandish heroism are a

foundation   but   in their forgetfulness   they

rot the good

fragrant and verdant flowers strewn as a carpet upon the
city streets

the mother and child weeping graveside at a

valiant husband and father are not honoured and
consoled

in the village   a spear thrust towards a vile foreign foe

breaks in pieces to the cheers of traitorous cowards

realising nothing   fools   teach no one

                    self indulgent boy   who are
                    you to peer down from
                    such heights

rage at others as much as you like if you imagine it
serves a

good and definable end   but sharpen your mind also
to this

thought   those you ruthlessly pull apart are doing the

best they can   had you not embraced them   and they
you

is this not enough

            it is as if my smile were a mask   as if i
            have been pushed onto a stage   and am now

            acting in a grotesque drama   i am not

            ready for the disquiet of questions i

            cannot yet put into words i am possessed

            of a crisis my friends do not help me escape

your indignation is not with who they are or with what

they do   are you not embarrassed at how you diminish

your spirit   with an uncompromising nature you persist

in ruinous self-pity and shamefully trouble the

doubtless value of your present and perfect time

it is a fine and noble skill

for the freed soul to ask without an urgent

need for an answer or response

what is so obscured that the deliberate commitment
of incising a word or thought onto a papyrus

would not expose

mine   alongside his   here   in front of me

> *and someday   when an able diligent scribe*

> *attends his business   my students yours*

suppose the utterance of a word can be compared to an

actor   entering a scene at a crucial moment   in costume

line ready he instead   breaks all convention

does nothing   nothing at all

the audience   seized with discomfort   expect

comedy   drama conflict resolution   but

he goes on   signifies   standing

mysteriously   this is itself a destination   and

while our young exemplar

proceeds   somewhere

he fails to go   there   wisely

certainly here

on the outskirts of his text   reclaim an advantage he
lacks

we recognise those tangled tortured paths of his
reasoning

those blockages in his imagination

our duty is to escape from them

but with this portion he here provides   might we affect

an understanding   reference measure out a
perseverance

as if it were a star   one plucked from amongst that
multitude
and   should we then wonder   are we then ready to
build a

consequence transpiring around this event   the exact

one now happening to us

they judge little   if at all

my companions   this hard hard land   this hard

doubt ravaged land   this doubt bitten land

how has it touched them

how has it touched me

but we   like a recluse on a mountain side

are hidden away

edged out of obscurity

the austere mood he beckons us towards
is itself a perspective   an ancient   clutched after thing

the struggle then is to name   to reckon with

those particular sensations coursing through the body

we may picture the delirium produced by this
experience
as two strangers   perhaps meeting for the first time
each

longs to flesh out the most elemental   proper and

fitting language to question what each has finally

ceased evading so as to restore to the world's opulence

its primal   startling   original immensity of instantaneous
awe

in him   we find there is a spirit of recovery

melancholy are those early morning flames
that are music to their speech

the wandering that is their end

as one

do they see   do they feel

these lively   these pulsing forms

as red   as solid and as true   as any knowable

thing   each flicker teases out the telling of a

new   or old way of being   is a song of motion

men and women have   alike   come to praise

there amongst this communion   there

and there again   the succour   they

come to warm themselves by

is   to them   an adequate compensation   an affected

working out of a morning   time for them is an imagined

glow of readiness   and to accept or deny any phenomenal
or at least promissory word of loving sacrifice is to root

themselves in its expository capacity   would that their

encounter seem for a whole year like armour to them

because   against its insults a self   assured and

paraphrased   is a fairness of presented decorum not

one soul ever entirely approaches

but   what do i mean by this

i mean   for myself   what do i mean

could it be

that the ambition of daylight is to satisfy a blade of grass

seen through the cracked stones of an old wall

a poem carries within its body the presence of other poems

following the image it names   a word is to the speaker what

he feels   is tantalisingly remote   partially explicable

oceanic   he says   oceanic

of the tension he wishes to alleviate by illustration bound as it is to earthly things   suppose

a horse on the plain   races   his mane lifts his

praises to the clouds   a soldier   flexes his arm

deliberates his aim   thrusts his spear to the

target   is freed victorious before any battle

all visions   childlike   return   statuesque and
legendary

to mortal glimmerings
and are taken away again

but

this is the pleasure of ruins

a function of the shadows they cast

why the mythical voicing of an abandonment

stated otherwise fits an ideal of the solid

alongside that of the imagined

why rugged objects   having come to us

laden with the acquired abundance of

the language of the time they inhabit

caution every confidence of those

who must draw near them

but   why is it they

and they alone   who

lift up   lift up

syllable by syllable

those words that haunt them with the
apocalyptic energy

of their delirious hiding away

but

more definite still

are those words and actions that   now destitute of

their creative potency by dreary overuse   reduce

a fearsome and provoking solitude to an exercise of

meager expectation with hardly enough substantive
power than that of a habitual meeting at a

threshold in the middle of a day

but we find there is in the seeing

from this plateau-like place the inevitably

melancholic magnitude of its continuity

its conditions   exposed as a lavishly absent symmetry

which   as it were

          mist-like

                                   newly rising

               burn away the disguises of its excess

soon   we may come to think
of two brothers

long estranged

apprehended   identified with   this regret anchors
them

they are now a servant to those too easily counted

          phrases   experiences

each says   has said   perhaps   to   for years

is it true to claim that a unity is healed by the precision

of the disaster it is forced to confront

is it they   and possibly we with them   who   burdened at such

knowledge   sail off in separate boats   voyagers to some

distant continent crippled after a hyperbolic earthquake

those storm lashed forces   those upturned hands protecting nothing

dull houses of reed and clay greet the newcomers   how quickly

they neglect the texture of any left behind thing   what can

stay to become a poetry for them yet   but an affecting

monotone ecstasy is a chant of divine interest and it

pulses its personality throughout the streets like a common heart come out   come out to where they are

distinguish day from day

firm up that soil

that book buried book finishes its form   there
                    diliose

Acknowledgements

jesus, thank you for this life. being a poet is beautiful. thank you everyone at aos publishing. i am grateful to my family for their support over the years, especially to mom for typing out much of the book. my writing friends in calgary are a constant blessing, and I love you: matt smith, weyman chan, vivian hansen, cecilia frey and john, pam medland, sharon butala, julie sedivy and ian, sarah x murphy, rob trawick and lee desjardins. ah, friends of my youth, i love you: tim goode and joelle, ian and vicki duiven, dan poxon and amy, lloyd and kimberly farley, jamie and hannah stroud, mike and vicki coverdale, rob jagodginski. the alberta foundation for the arts awarded me a generous individual artists' project grant in 2019. the grant made it possible for me to return to the leighton artists' studios at the banff centre for the arts. i am deeply grateful to everyone at the banff centre for creating a sanctuary for artists. my many residences there over the years have been a blessing to me, and i ache to return every day. in january 2022 i was the writer in residence at the wallace stegner house in eastend, saskatchewan. it was there i finished "the commune of our waking ". my month long residency in the house opened my spirit. thank you eastend arts council for choosing me to be your writer in residence. it was an honour and a joy. my church families at saint laurence, calgary, and saint johns, Edmonton ,bless my soul. sharla, my companion on the journey, i love you! jesus, thanks!

Author Bio

stuart ian mckay is a calgary based poet. his poetry and non fiction have been published in many canadian literary journals and anthologies. "stele of several ladies-a long poem "a cognate of prayer ",his first two books of poetry, were published in 2005 and 2013 by passwords enterprises, an independent calgary press." even the idea of maya is maya ",a poetry chapbook, was published by frog hollow press in victoria in 2019 as part of its dis/ability series. stuart is the editor of "the way out is the way in", a chapbook celebrating the work of canadian poets with disabilities, published by the league of canadian poets in 2022. stuart and fellow calgary poet/noise and sound artist matt smith comprise the poetry creation and performance team "the thornlake endeavour". stuart serves on the poetry editorial collective of filling station. he is the alberta/ north west territories' representative for the league of canadian poets. in january 2022 he was the writer in residence at the wallace stegner house in eastend, saskatchewan.